beauty
trix
for
COOL CHIX

beauty trix

for
COOL CHIX

easy-to-make lotions, potions, and spells
to bring out a beautiful you

Caroline Naylor

Watson-Guptill Publications/New York

First published in the United States in 2003 by
Watson-Guptill Publications,
a division of VNU Business Media, Inc.
770 Broadway, New York, NY 10003
www.watsonguptill.com

PRODUCED BY Breslich & Foss Ltd, London
DESIGNED BY Roger Daniels

Illustrations by Debbie Boone
Text by Caroline Naylor
Photos pages 48-55, 80-87 by Shona Wood
Hand model: Emma Davys

Special thanks to the cool chix in Sal Pernice's jazz dance class
for their ideas, suggestions, and enthusiasm.

Library of Congress Cataloging-in-Publication Data

Naylor, Caroline.
  Beauty trix for cool chix : easy-to-make lotions, potions, and spells
to bring out a beautiful you / Caroline Naylor.
    p. cm.
  ISBN 0-8230-6957-5
  I.   Title.

                                                    2003106626

Printed and bound in China

ISBN 0-8230-6957-5

1 2 3 4 5 6 7 8 / 10 09 08 07 06 05 04 03

Every effort has been made to ensure that the information presented is accurate.
Readers are strongly advised to read product labels, follow manufacturers' instructions,
and heed warnings. The publisher disclaims any liability for injuries, losses, untoward results,
or any other damages that may result from the use of the information in this book.

Contents

Getting

We all know that real beauty comes from within, and that to look your glowing best you should eat well and drink plenty of water. But who doesn't need a little extra boost from time to time? Every gal needs a bag of beauty trix, and that's where we come in. You'll have a great time making the potions and perfumes described in this book—all easy to make and designed to bring out a beautiful you!

Started

You'll find recipes to pamper your hands and feet, tips on looking after your hair and styling it for party glamour (or just giving it a quick change for every day), and glittery treats to make your skin and hair sparkle. You'll learn about essential oils and how you can use them to change your mood (whether you want to feel on top of the world or as cool as a cucumber), and about beauty emergency secrets for those not-so-perfect days. There's even a chapter on decorating bottles, jars, and boxes so you can store your handmade potions in style!

All of the recipes are made with natural ingredients that can be bought at supermarkets and health stores, so there are no dangerous chemicals to deal with. However, as natural ingredients contain no preservatives, these recipes won't last forever—about two weeks if kept in a cool fridge—so don't go making masses of the stuff or it'll just go to waste.

The recipes will not only do your looks a power of good, but they're easy to make and fun, too! So why not ask a few girlfriends over for a special beauty day, or cook up a batch of your favorite scent, pour it into little decorated bottles, and give them as gifts?

Before you begin, take a minute to read the

Serious Stuff section on pages 10–11. Then say good-bye to bad hair days, dull skin, scruffy nails, and yucky feet, and hello to the world of sleek glamour and sensational style! What are you waiting for?

Serious

Listen up! Whether you're cooking and storing a batch of beauty treats, or trying an ingredient for the first time, it's important to follow a few simple safety rules.

1. Some of the recipes will ask you to heat ingredients in the microwave or on the stove. **ALWAYS** make sure an adult is around to help. This yellow sign will remind you.

2. Before using any new ingredient on your skin (such as eyelash glue, or anything you haven't used before), test a little on the inside of your wrist and then leave it overnight. If the area itches in the morning, don't use that ingredient because your skin doesn't like it and it could give you a rash!

3. Always sterilize jars or bottles before using them to hold your precious potions. Even if they

Stuff

look clean, they might contain dirt that could contaminate your new recipes and make them go moldy. Just follow these simple steps to clean any glass or plastic container:

To sterilize glass bottles and jars:

1. Heat oven to 150°F (50°C).

2. Wash jars and lids thoroughly in hot, soapy water.

3. Place jars and bottles on their sides on the racks in the pre-heated oven.

4. Leave for ten minutes, then remove using oven gloves.

To sterilize plastic containers:

1. Place containers in a microwave-safe bowl and cover with water. Micro- wave on high for 1 minute at a time until water starts to boil (or place in a saucepan, cover with water, and bring gently to a boil on the stove).

2. Boil for three minutes.

3. Use oven gloves to take the bowl out of the microwave (or the saucepan off of the stove). Lift containers out with tongs and leave them to dry on kitchen towels.

Potions

In this section you'll find simple recipes for making your own sweet-scented perfumes and bath oils and, for the best pout in town, our lovely lip balm. You'll also find advice about magical essential oils—what they are, and how they can be used to make you feel fabulous.

Some of the ingredients in this section, such as the essential oils, can be found at drugstores. Others, like the base oils for the perfumes and bath oils, are carried in health stores. Essential oils range in price, depending on how pure they are—but don't go nuts and spend all of your savings! You can use the cheaper ones for these recipes and they'll still smell just as good.

So get sniffing, mixing, and casting your magic and soon you'll feel on top of the world!

& Spells

Mix up some mood magic!

Perfect Pout Potion

Your skin produces its own oil, which is why your nose or forehead might get shiny sometimes. Unfortunately, your lips don't (how selfish of them!), so they can get really dry, especially in the winter. Pamper your lips with this simple and delicious recipe.

You will need:

- 2 teaspoons coconut oil
- 1 teaspoon beeswax
- small microwave-safe bowl (or double boiler if using the stove)
- wooden spoon
- your favorite food flavoring
- tiny container with lid (an old eye shadow container with screw-on top would be perfect)

1. Place oil and beeswax in the bowl. Heat in the micro-wave on high for 1 minute at a time until it's all melted (or place in double boiler and melt over high heat on the stove).

2. Using oven gloves, remove from the microwave or stove. Stir the mixture.

3. Add a couple drops of food flavoring—vanilla? peppermint? strawberry? (yum!). Stir until just warm to the touch.

4. Pour into a clean container. Leave until cool and firm to the touch (it should be slightly firmer than Vaseline). Cover only when the lip balm is completely cold. Then pucker up!

Serious Stuff!

Always allow the recipe you are making to cool completely before sealing it in its container. If you don't do this, condensation will form and ruin your wonderful potion.

Personalized Perfume

There's no need to spend a fortune on expensive French perfume to smell your best. Just follow our simple recipe, then add your favorite essential oil (orange, rose, sandalwood, musk—whatever does it for you) to make your very own personal scent.

You will need:

- unscented base oil, such as wheatgerm, avocado, or almond oil
- coffee-cup saucer or egg cup
- essential oil
- teaspoon
- dropper
- plastic wrap
- small funnel
- small bottle

1. Measure 2 teaspoons of the base oil into the saucer or egg cup.

2. Add a few drops of essential oil, or try one of the scent spell recipes on pages 18-19. Stir after adding each drop.

3. Cover with plastic wrap and leave to blend for 12 hours in a cool, dark place. Then pour it into a bottle using the funnel.

Bathing Beauty Oil

After a hard day hanging out with your friends, relax and unwind in a lovely hot bath with a few drops of fragrant bath oil. Mmmmm....

You will need:
- ¼ cup (60 ml) treated castor oil (pure and odorless)
- bottle with top
- small funnel
- essential oil

1. Using the funnel, pour the castor oil into the bottle.

2. Add a few drops of essential oil, or one of the scent spell recipes on pages 18-19, stirring after each drop.

3. When you are happy with the scent, cover the bottle tightly and shake well. Leave the oil to mature for a week, then use one tablespoon for each luxurious bathing experience.

Hot Tip

If you prefer bubbles, add a few drops of your favorite essential oil to ¼ cup (60 ml) baby shampoo and pour under a running tap.

Scent Spells

Essential oils are magical: They can actually help change your moods. Lavender, for instance, is very calming, so it's good to use in bath oils for a relaxing soak. Lemon, on the other hand, can wake you up! So cast a spell with these special scents, each of which can be added to the basic perfume recipe (page 16), bath oil recipe (page 17), or any recipe that calls for essential oils.

SELF-ESTEEM

Does your confidence need a boost? Maybe you're going to a party and are feeling nervous that you won't know many people there? Add a few drops of this deliciously spicy combo to the basic perfume recipe and you'll feel like the belle of the ball.

You will need:
- 5 drops ylang ylang oil
- 4 drops rose oil
- 3 drops lime oil

HAPPINESS

If you're feeling a little down, this rosy recipe will put a smile back on your face. The main oil in this potion is rose, which is used in lots of expensive perfumes. Teamed with zingy lemon and bergamot oils, this fragrance will put a spring in your step in no time.

You will need:
- 5 drops rose oil
- 4 drops lemon oil
- 3 drops bergamot oil

VITALITY

The mix of oils in this recipe makes you feel relaxed yet wide awake and ready to tackle anything. The main scent is carnation oil, which can make you feel healthy and energetic.

You will need:

- 6 drops carnation oil
- 2 drops lemon verbena oil
- 3 drops sandalwood oil

RELAXATION

Everyone feels stressed out sometimes, but this mixture will help you feel calm and relaxed. Use it in a relaxing bath before bed, or sprinkle a couple of drops on your pillow at night for the sweetest of dreams.

You will need:

- 6 drops sandalwood oil
- 4 drops orange oil
- 1 drop pine oil

ATTRACTION

Is there a crush you'd like to cast a spell over? If so, this is the fragrance for you. It'll make you feel calm and confident, so you can bewitch the boy of your dreams!

You will need:

- 7 drops jasmine oil
- 3 drops orange oil

HARMONY

his spell uses an oil called ylang ang, which makes you feel calm; ergamot, which makes you feel right and confident; and vanilla, hich smells warm and sweet.

You will need:

- 2 drops ylang ylang oil
- 2 drops bergamot oil
- 1 drop vanilla oil

COURAGE

This sweet and spicy spell is a mix of bergamot (for confidence), jasmine (for strength), and grapefruit oil (for perkiness!).

You will need:

- 5 drops bergamot oil
- 2 drops jasmine oil
- 1 drop grapefruit oil

Love Quiz

Where are you in the romance stakes? Take this quiz (no cheating), then read your score to see which potion recipe is right for you!

1. You've had a crush on a cute boy in school all year and you're desperate for him to notice you. Do you:
- a) Hide every time you see him coming and then kick yourself for being so shy?
- b) Smile at him in class and then go bright red and die of embarrassment?
- c) Decide that the boy is going to be yours, march up to him at the next opportunity, and ask him out?

2. Which of the following describes you best?
- a) All of your friends are girls, and you feel nervous and uncomfortable talking to boys.
- b) Most of your friends are girls, but you do have one or two boy friends, mostly from first grade.
- c) You hang out with a big crowd of boys and girls and you feel just as comfortable with both.

3. At last, your crush has asked you on a date, and it's today!!! Have you:
- a) Spent the whole week worrying about what to wear and shopping for a cool new outfit?
- b) Been window shopping, but in the end decided on something you already have that looks good and feels comfortable?
- c) Left it until the last minute, then thrown on the nearest pair of jeans? (Why worry? You're gorgeous!)

4. It's your boyfriend's birthday and he's asked you to a family party to meet the folks for the first time. When you arrive do you:
- a) Cling to his arm feeling terrified, then lose all ability to speak?
- b) Feel shy but still try to relax and be chatty?
- c) Quickly make friends with everyone and have yourself a ball?

5. You have a huge, secret crush on your friend's big brother. Do you:
- a) Avoid her house like the plague, until she thinks she's done something wrong?
- b) Turn up at her house as much as normal, but dive under-cover whenever you see him coming?
- c) Spend so much time at her house, following him around, that her parents are worried you might have moved in?

6. Your brother has a group of friends over listening to music in his room. You need to go and ask him something. Do you:
- a) Decide it can wait and stay out of sight until they've all gone home?
- b) Knock shyly on the door until your brother comes out to see you?
- c) Barge straight in, give his friends a wave, then turn off the music and speak to your brother?

Your score:

Mostly As:
You could be lucky in love, but you need to be more confident about yourself first! You're gorgeous, funny, and smart, so believe in all of your good points and let them shine through! Try our Self-Esteem spell (page 18) to give yourself a boost, then go out and wow those boys!

Mostly Bs:
You're trying, but you're still a little shy around those cute boys. When you talk to them, you panic! Believe it or not, they are nervous, too. Try making the first move and you'll be surprised how well it can go. For a little extra help, dab on our Courage spell (page 19).

Mostly Cs:
Shy and nervous are two words that least describe you. You're not afraid of anyone! Be yourself, but make sure you slow down enough to be sensitive to those around you or you might scare boys away. Our fabulous Relaxation spell (page 19) could be just the thing!

Locks

It's best to have your hair trimmed—whether or not you're trying to grow it out—at least once every six weeks. This will keep split ends under control and keep your hair looking sleek. Everything else you can do at home!

Give your hair some tender loving care.

Just turn the page for a whole bunch of simple treatments—everything from your very own shampoos and conditioners to a gentle herbal rinse that will give your natural color a teensy lift. There are even tips for you curly-haired beauties on looking after your ringlets and perking them up for parties. So don't hide that head of hair under a hat—make the most of your crowning glory!

Herbal Fix-it Shampoo

Did you know that the right herb can do wonders for problem hair? Just pick your problem from the list at right to see which herb you need, then mix up a batch of shampoo and give your hair a treat!

Dry hair: parsley

Oily hair: rosemary

Damaged/colored/permed hair: chamomile (for light hair) or sage (for dark hair)

You will need:

- microwave-safe bowl with lid (or saucepan with cover if using the stove)
- 2/3 cup (150 ml) unscented or baby shampoo
- 1 tablespoon dried or 3 tablespoons fresh chopped chosen herb
- 1 cup (250 ml) water
- sieve
- bowl
- container with lid

1. Place the water and your herb of choice in the bowl and microwave on high for 1 minute at a time until it begins to boil, or place herbs and water in a saucepan and bring to a boil over high heat on the stove.

2. Using oven gloves, remove from microwave or stove. Cover mixture and leave to cool. Once cool, strain the liquid through the sieve into bowl.

3. Pour the shampoo into your container and add 1/3 cup (80 ml) of the herbal liquid. Cover and shake well.

4. Use as ordinary shampoo. This will keep for two months.

Once Over Lightly

Don't eat those eggs—put them in your shampoo! Egg helps give body to fine hair. And you can even add your favorite scent to make this shampoo special. Don't make more than enough for one wash, though, because it won't keep and you'll end up smelling like a rotten egg (bad joke, sorry!).

You will need:
- 1 egg
- small bowl
- fork
- 4 tablespoons unscented or baby shampoo
- essential oil(s)

1. Crack egg into bowl and beat with a fork until fluffy.

2. Add shampoo and essential oils (see Scent Spells, pages 18–19).

3. Beat with fork until blended.

4. Use right away as you would normal shampoo.

Super Sculpting Wax

Want to give your hair a glamorous new look? Or maybe your everyday style won't do as it's told? Just apply a tiny amount of this super sculpting wax to dry hair, then sculpt into the style of your dreams!

You will need:
- ¼ cup (60 ml) beeswax
- microwave-safe bowl (or double boiler if using the stove)
- wooden spoon
- ½ cup (125 ml) vegetable oil
- 1 teaspoon essential oil
- container with lid

1. Place the beeswax in the bowl and microwave on high for 45 seconds at a time until it has melted (or place in a double boiler and melt over low heat on the stove).

2. Use oven gloves to remove mixture from the microwave or stove. Stir in the vegetable oil. If you want a scent, add an essential oil or your favorite scent spell (see pages 18-19).

3. Stir to mix. Before it cools, pour into a container. When it has cooled completely (this could take up to two hours), screw on the lid. This mixture will keep for two weeks.

Lemon Rinse

Lemon is great for oily hair, so if you're always fighting the battle of the grease, this lemon rinse is for you. Other citrus fruits will work, too—try oranges, limes, or grapefruit.

You will need:
- juice of 1 lemon
- 1 cup (250 ml) warm water
- tall glass

1. Mix water and lemon juice in glass.

2. Lean over the sink or tub (or stand in the shower) and rinse through freshly shampooed hair.

3. Leave for 3 minutes, then rinse with water.

Instant Shampoo

If you've made your favorite Scent Spell (pages 18-19), all you have to do is mix it with some unscented shampoo to make your own special hair brew.

You will need:
- 2/3 cup (150 ml) unscented or baby shampoo
- 1 teaspoon of your favorite scent spell (pages 18-19)
- jar or bottle with screw-on top

1. Pour shampoo into clean jar or bottle.

2. Add scent spell (using funnel if bottle opening is narrow).

3. Screw on top and shake well. (Always shake before using.)

Heavenly Hair Wrap

If your crowning glory is more straw than silk, try this rich conditioning treatment, good for all hair types. Soon you'll be the sleekest girl in school!

1. Mix all the ingredients in a bowl.

2. Wet your hair so it's damp (but not dripping wet). Wet your hands and apply the mixture to your damp hair.

3. Wrap your head in a towel and go do something relaxing for about 15 minutes.

4. Take off the towel and shampoo as usual. Your hair will smell divine and be as soft as silk when dry!

Avocado Conditioner

Avocados are bursting with richness that your hair will love. You should probably skip this recipe if you've got oily hair, but it will work wonders for those with dry to normal hair and scalps.

You will need:
- towel
- 1 ripe avocado
- knife
- spoon
- fork
- 4 tablespoons (60 ml) vegetable oil
- bowl

1. Warm your towel in the drier, or by draping it over a heater.

2. Cut the avocado in half and gently twist the two halves apart. Remove the pit and scoop out the flesh.

3. Mash up the avocado with a fork in the bowl. Then beat in the oil.

4. When you have a fairly smooth mixture, massage it into your hair.

5. Wrap the warm towel around your hair and relax for 20 minutes.

6. Rinse your hair in warm water, then wash with a mild shampoo, such as the Instant Shampoo on page 27.

Cool Styles

Bored with the same old hairdo? Try these party styles to make your tresses look terrific. Better still, invite a friend over and do each other's hair!

Overnight Curls

Not everyone is blessed with a natural head of corkscrew curls, but don't worry...just fake it! If you start the night before, you can cook up a head of curls in no time!

1. Wash your hair the night before the day you want the style.

2. Towel dry your hair.

3. While it is still damp, begin braiding your hair. You can do as many or as few braids as you like.

4. Sleep on the braids. When you wake up and undo them, you'll have the curls you always dreamed of!

Zigzag Hair Part

Here is an easy way for straight-haired girls to get a natural, tousled look. You can use almost any thin tool for this (but not a pen!).

1. Wet your hair so it's damp (not dripping wet).

2. Comb all of your hair forward so it's hanging over your forehead.

3. Take the pointed end of a comb and, starting at the back of your head, make a zigzag line moving forward toward your forehead. When you're done, the hair should fall to the right or left according to your zigzag.

Stylish Shortie

This style is great for short hair, or as a quick fix when you're trying to grow it out and it's getting on your nerves!

1. Brush your hair back away from your forehead.

2. Use a little hair gel to smooth hair back into a slick do.

3. Secure the loose ends under your favorite headband (to keep stray hairs from spoiling your sleek look), then slip on sparkly earrings for instant party glamour.

Color to Go

Give your natural hair color a helping hand with these healthy herbal rinses. They'll not only bring out the highlights of your own shade, but will make your hair ultra-shiny, too.

Warning!

These rinses can stain, so be sure to wear old clothes and use a towel you don't mind ruining. Probably best to check with the boss first!

FOR SULTRY DARK HAIR

you will need:

- 1 cup (250 ml) water
- microwave-safe bowl (or saucepan if using the stove)
- 1 tea bag (black, not green)
- 1 tablespoon dried sage
- sieve
- wooden spoon
- large bowl
- old towel

FOR FLAMING RED HAIR

you will need:

- 1 cup (250 ml) cranberry juice
- microwave-safe bowl (or saucepan if using the stove)
- 2 tablespoons dried sage
- sieve
- wooden spoon
- large bowl
- old towel

FOR FABULOUS FAIR HAIR

you will need:

- 1 cup (250 ml) water
- microwave-safe bowl (or saucepan if using the stove)
- 1 chamomile tea bag
- wooden spoon
- 1 tablespoon lemon juice
- large bowl
- old towel

Method for all three herbal brews:

1. Put the tea bags, herbs (if any), and water (or cranberry juice for redheads) in the bowl and microwave on high for 1 minute at a time until it boils. (Or bring to a boil in a saucepan over high heat on the stove.) Using oven gloves, remove from the microwave or stove. Let cool to room temperature.

2. Take out the tea bags and pour the mixture through a sieve if necessary to remove any herbs.

(Press down with the spoon to squeeze out all the liquid.) If you're making the rinse for fair hair, stir in the lemon juice.

3. Wash your hair as usual, then lean over the sink or tub and pour the brew over your hair. Use the extra bowl to catch the rinse and repeat four or five times. Wrap towel around your hair for 10 minutes, then rinse it with water.

Hair Mascara

You may have the healthiest, cleanest, sweetest-smelling hair in the world, but does it still need a little extra something? Of course it does, and hair mascara is just the thing! It will give you instant fun color that will stay put when you need it, but also wash out in a flash.

You will need:

- hair gel
- plate
- three or four colors of eye shadow
- spoon
- paper envelopes
- eyebrow brush

1. Place 3 or 4 blobs of hair gel on the plate, separate from each other.

2. Place a little of each eye shadow color into a separate paper envelope and crush it with the spoon until it turns into a powder.

3. Mix each color into one of the gel blobs, then use the eyebrow brush to coat locks of your hair. Let it dry, and voilà! Instant party sparkle!

Friendship Quiz

Have you got what it takes to be a best friend?

1. The boy you've had a crush on for ages asks you out for Saturday, but you've already made plans with your best friend. Do you:
   a) Say yes before he's even finished asking (your best friend won't mind—she knows you think he's cute!)?
   b) Tell him you'd love to, but you'll let him know later, then call your best friend and explain. If she's mad, tell her you'll turn him down?
   c) Tell him you've already got plans for Saturday, but what is he doing on Sunday?

2. You and your best friend have both been eyeing the coolest pair of jeans in your favorite store, but they're really expensive. Then you see them at half price, but there's only one pair left and it will fit both of you. Do you:
   a) Buy them for yourself (they'd look better on you anyway)?
   b) Buy them for yourself but tell her she can borrow them whenever she likes?
   c) Buy them for her (you already have plenty of jeans, and she'll be so happy!)?

3. You and your best friend both have a huge crush on a new boy in school. To your surprise, he comes over to you after class and asks you for a date. Do you:
   a) Say yes and think that your best friend will get over it (you can't help it if you're irresistible)?
   b) Tell him no, then tell your best friend all about it, being sure to point out how kind and unselfish you are?
   c) Turn him down nicely, but hint that your best friend thinks he's cute. Then don't breathe a word of it to her and see what happens?

4. Your best friend calls you Sunday night to say that she's finally kissed her secret crush, who happens to be hot property in school. The next day do you:
   a) Go to school early so you can be the first to spread the word?
   b) Tell the girls in your group, but swear them all to secrecy?
   c) Don't tell anyone (your best friend would be so embarrassed)?

5. You get some money for your birthday and can't wait to spend all day at the mall shopping. Then your best friend asks you to come with her to visit her sick cousin instead. Do you:
- a) Laugh out loud, ask her if she's lost her mind, then get back to thinking about some serious shopping?
- b) Sigh, then say okay, but can she make it quick so you can still get to the mall?
- c) Say yes right away. You know you'll have fun with your best friend wherever you are, and the new clothes can wait?

6. You and your best friend are going to a party and she's stressed out over what to wear. Do you:
- a) Tell her to wear that baggy shirt and an old pair of jeans (you don't want her to look better than you)?
- b) Go through her closet with her and try and find something that might look okay?
- c) Lend her your brand new skirt and skinny tee. You know she loves them and she'll look terrific!

Your score:

Mostly As:
And you call yourself a best friend?! You're lucky she's stuck with you for this long. Being a good pal means caring and sharing and not just thinking about yourself. Take the time to mix up some special beauty potions for your best bud and present them in pretty bottles you've made yourself.

Mostly Bs:
You think a lot of your pal, but sometimes when the going gets tough, you get going! Try to be there when she needs you and she'll realize you are the one she can always count on. Suggest a beauty day at your house with just the two of you, and mix up some fragrant brews!

Mostly Cs
You are almost too good to be true! You are totally unselfish and your best friend knows she can always count on you. Just make sure that it goes both ways. Drop some hints about your favorite scent and see if she goes out of her way to whip up something especially for you.

Cute Paws

It's all very well looking after your hair, face, and body, but what about your poor hands and feet? Hands get a rough deal in life: They're out in all weather working hard, getting wet, and the most they can expect in return is a dab of hand cream once in a while. And your feet? Trampled on all day long, squished into your favorite shoes— and they don't even get the hand cream treatment! Well, it's all about to change....

Get ready to roar with these treats for hands and feet!

& Sweet Feet

Tootsie Treat

Give yourself a toe-tapping tingle with this lavish foot oil—it'll soothe away tiredness, leave your feet smelling sweet, and make you want to dance all night!

> ### You will need:
> · ½ cup (125 ml) vegetable oil
> · bottle or jar with lid
> · 6 drops peppermint oil
> · towel

1. Pour the vegetable oil into a clean bottle or jar.

2. Add the peppermint oil. Put lid on bottle and shake well.

3. Before bed, soak your feet in warm water for 5 minutes, then dry them on the towel and massage a little oil into your tootsies. Slip on a pair of socks to sleep in, and you'll wake up with completely new feet—well, they'll still be your old feet, but they'll feel great!

Sugar Smoothie

Treat your hands and feet to a relaxing sugar scrub! This clever mixture works perfectly because the oil helps soften rough skin, while the sugar scrubs it away. Your dry skin won't stand a chance! Best of all, the mixture will keep for 6-12 months for lots of skin pampering.

You will need:
- ½ cup (125 ml) sugar
- ¼ cup (60 ml) olive or vegetable oil
- 7 drops essential oil or your favorite scent spell from pages 18-19 (optional)
- bowl
- spoon

1. Put sugar and oil in a bowl and mix until it feels pasty. Stir in the essential oils, if using.

2. Sit on the edge of the tub. Rub the mixture gently into your hands and feet, especially over rough spots like your heels. Then rinse off. Follow with a dab of moisturizer or the Tootsie Treat, shown opposite.

Warning!
The oil in this mixture can leave the bottom of the bathtub slippery. Make sure you clean the tub carefully when you're done so no one takes a dive!

Pampering Paw Cream

Have you been washing the dishes again? Well, that's very helpful, but it can make your hands feel dry and rough. Give your paws a purrr-fect treat with this homemade hand cream.

You will need:
- ¾ cup (200 ml) petroleum jelly (such as Vaseline)
- ½ cup (125 ml) beeswax
- microwave-safe bowl (or double boiler if using the stove)
- wooden spoon
- 1 teaspoon unscented base oil, such as wheatgerm, avocado, or almond
- your favorite essential oil
- funnel
- bottle with top

1. Place the petroleum jelly and the beeswax in the microwave-safe bowl and cook on high for 1 minute at a time, stirring every minute until it's thoroughly melted. If using the stove, place jelly and beeswax in double boiler and melt slowly over low heat.

2. When the mixture is thoroughly melted, use oven gloves to remove from microwave or stove. Stir in the base oil and some drops of your favorite essential oil.

3. Let mixture cool completely, then pour it through the funnel into a nice clean bottle. Shake well, then massage a little into your hands for skin you can be proud of!

Manicure in Minutes

If you've never given yourself a manicure, you'll be amazed at what a difference it makes. It's even better if you get a friend to help, so you can sit back and relax while your hands get the Hollywood treatment.

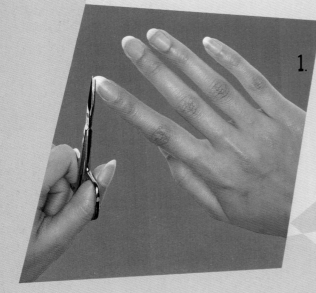

1. Carefully cut each nail, starting from the side and working toward the middle, until it is the length you like. Cut all of your nails to the same length.

2. Using the lighter side of the nail file, carefully pull it a few times over the edge of each nail, working from the side to the center to form a smooth edge. Take a big blob of hand cream, such as the Pampering Paw Cream (page 42), and massage it into your hands until it is almost all gone. Then blot your hands and nails with a tissue.

3. Paint your nails with a base coat and leave it to dry completely.

4. Apply two coats of your favorite nail polish, leaving it to dry between coats. Now slip on some glittery rings and go show off those cute claws!

Perfect Pedicure

Get your feet in top form with this luxury pedicure. **Try to do this every two weeks and before you know it you'll have baby-soft feet.**

Warning!

Many a pedicure has come to a tragic end by putting shoes on too soon. Make sure your polish is rock-hard before doing so! If you have to go out before your polish is completely dry, wear a pair of flip-flops or sandals and hope for the best.

You will need:

- bowl of warm soapy water
- towel
- pumice stone
- hand cream
- nail scissors or clippers
- nail file
- cotton balls
- clear base coat
- nail polish

1. Soak your feet in a bowl of warm, soapy water, then dry them thoroughly with a nice fluffy towel.

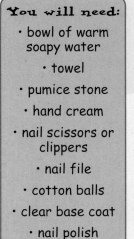

2. Use the pumice stone to gently rub off any dried skin around your heels and toes. This can be tricky if you're ticklish!

3. Rub scented hand cream into your new soft feet (try our Tootsie Treat, page 40, or the Pampering Paw Cream, page 42).

4. Cut your toenails straight across. Then use the nail file to smooth down the corners.

5. Separate your toes with cotton balls. Paint on a layer of base coat, then two coats of polish. Make sure you let each coat dry thoroughly before applying the next one. After the final coat, go barefoot or wear sandals for the next few hours until the polish has hardened.

Creative

Bored with your plain old nails? Got a new outfit and can't find the right color nail polish? You've come to the right place, because here you'll find ways to turn your nails into tiny works of art. If you have magic fingers, you can cut out all sorts of tiny pics from magazines and glue them right onto your nails. If you're less good at fine fingerwork, you can use tiny stickers or bright sequins

Claws

instead—or just shake on some glitter!
You can even mix your
very own nail polish
color, using a tiny
bit of eye shadow
(ask first if it's your
sister's), and have fun
with a rainbow
of different
colors. And
don't forget,
each of these
looks can be
used on toes, too!

Dazzling Decoupage

Nail transfers and stickers are great for fun nails, but if you want something totally different, cut out little pictures or strips from a magazine and stick them onto your nails.

1. First, decide which picture you want on which nail, then lay them out in order on the table.

2. Pick up the first picture and dab a dot of clear polish on the back. Carefully place the picture on your nail and press gently. Repeat for the other pictures, then leave the polish to dry.

3. Carefully apply one coat of clear polish to each nail. When your nails are completely dry (be patient!), apply a coat of glitter polish for a bit of added sparkle.

Create-a-Color

Create your own unique nail polish with just clear polish and eye shadow or powder blusher in your favorite color. **M**ake a whole bottle of one color, or little bits of lots of colors. **Y**ou can even build your own personal line of nail polish with fun names for each color!

You will need:

- eye shadow or powder blusher
- small plastic baggie
- spoon
- scissors
- clear nail polish
- nail polish remover
- disposable cup (optional)

1. Scoop out a little eye shadow or blusher and put into the baggie. Crush it to a fine powder with the back of the spoon.

2. Snip off a corner of the baggie to make a small funnel.

3. Pour a little powder into the bottle of clear polish (or into a bit of polish in a cup). Stir with the applicator brush, adding more powder to get the color you want. If the mix gets too thick, add two drops of remover. Then apply! (If you have clear polish left, clean the brush with remover and replace.)

Candy Stripes

Heading for a picnic on a summer day? Candy-striped nails are what you need! It's simple to get the effect with plain white polish and your favorite bright pink or red. Here's how.

You will need:
- white nail polish
- bright pink or red nail polish
- tiny paintbrush
- nail polish remover
- tissues

1. Apply two layers of white polish, allowing each coat to dry thoroughly.

2. Using the tiny brush, carefully apply two to three stripes of red polish across each nail.

3. Pour a small amount of polish remover into the bottle cap and clean the brush by swishing it in the remover and then wiping it off with a tissue.

4. Add a second coat of red to each stripe. Allow to dry thoroughly.

Spring Flowers

Turn your hands into a bouquet of spring flowers! This is a perfect look for cheering yourself up in the middle of winter, when spring seems a million miles away.

1. Apply two coats of the light pink polish. Let each coat dry thoroughly.

2. Using your paintbrush, apply a yellow or gold dot in the center of each nail.

3. Pour a small amount of polish remover into the bottle cap and clean the brush by swishing it in the remover and then wiping it clean with a tissue.

4. Using your clean brush, apply pink or red dots in a circle around each yellow center. Allow to dry thoroughly.

Stick-on Stunners

There are all kinds of exotic gems, sequins, stickers, and temporary tattoos available to decorate your nails. Just apply your favorite polish and stick 'em on!

1. Apply one coat of clear polish, then two coats of your favorite color. Let each coat dry thoroughly before applying the next.

2. Apply a drop of nail glue to each nail and press the sticker, gem, or transfer on top.

3. Allow to dry completely. Finish off with one coat of clear nail polish.

Instant Glitter Nails

Here is a simple, fast way to get some glitter into your life. You only need nail polish (any color will do) and some glitter to shake on top.

1. Cover your work surface with newspaper (glitter goes everywhere).

2. Apply a layer of clear or colored polish to one nail and, holding your hand over the newspaper, quickly shake glitter onto the wet polish. The glitter will stick to the polished surface but hopefully not to anything else.

3. Continue to apply polish, then glitter, to each nail until both hands are done.

4. When absolutely dry, add a layer of clear polish to keep the glitter in place.

Astro Quiz

Are you hot and fiery, natural and earthy, quirky and airy, or as cool as water?

1. Which is your favorite lip gloss color?
   a) Deep reds and pinks (they make you look older and feel confident).
   b) Anything, as long as it has loads of glitter in it.
   c) You don't wear gloss, just a slick of balm when your lips are dry.
   d) A glossy, pale pink.

2. What is the one accessory you won't leave home without?
   a) Shades, even in the rain.
   b) Your huge-rimmed, funky, floppy hat.
   c) A backpack that holds everything you could ever need.
   d) A silver necklace that your grandmother gave you.

3. What does your dresser have on top of it (be honest!)?
   a) Most of it is covered by a fluffy red feather boa. The rest is so full of junk you can never find anything in a hurry.
   b) China poodles and stuff you get from thrift stores.
   c) Just a few seashells and maybe a sports trophy or two.
   d) It's full of framed photographs of your family and friends.

4. How do you like to wear your hair?
   a) Short and spiky, and you love to experiment with colors.
   b) In any old style, as long as you're wearing ribbons or a bright scarf.
   c) Short and easy. You can't be bothered with complicated styles.
   d) Long, flowing, and always brushed.

5. How would you describe the way you dress?
   a) Loud and proud! You like to stand out in a crowd and be the center of attention.
   b) You like to look a bit different from everyone else. You are happiest in vintage bargains that you dress up with sequins and cool buttons.
   c) You like easy t-shirts, jeans, and sweats whenever possible.
   d) You love flowing skirts, shirts, and dresses that are comfortable but still funky.

6. What is the one beauty product that you always take with you on vacation?
   a) Red lip gloss.
   b) Glitter polish for your toes.
   c) High-protection sunscreen.
   d) Bath oil.

Your score:

Mostly As:
You are hot and spicy with more of the fire element in your personality than any of the other three elements. You are bold, confident, and a bit of a show-off, but your friends (and you have lots of them) think you're tons of fun! You'll love all of our bright and beautiful beauty treats, but the ones you really should try are the Hair Mascara (page 34) and Color to Go (page 32), as you love to cause a stir!

Mostly Bs:
You are a quirky chick, with the air element dominating your beauty personality. You have your own personal style and will wear anything, whatever the fashion, as long as it catches your eye and makes you stand out in a crowd. You will love our Glitter City section (pages 58–67), because you believe that a girl can never have too much sparkle in her life!

Mostly Cs:
You are an earth girl, which means you are natural and not showy. You don't like too much attention, and you are happier going for walks in jeans and a t-shirt than shopping for hours in a crowded mall. You are definitely not a beauty junkie, and you let your natural charm shine through with your warm personality. If this is you, you'll love all our totally natural recipes, but especially the Perfect Pout Potion (page 14).

Mostly Ds:
You are a dreamy water mermaid who likes to go with the flow. You love to shimmer in cool shades of blue, white, and pale green, and you won't wear anything that isn't comfy (so high heels are definitely out!). Your friends and family mean the world to you, and in return they know they can depend on your kind and steady nature. Head straight for our Bathing Beauty Oil (page 17)—there's nothing you like better than a long, hot bath.

Glitter

What's a girl to do when she needs some sparkle in her life? Glitterize, that's what! You can give your hair, skin, and face some extra dazzle in an instant with the ideas in this special section. Make your own glitter hair gel, create an entrance with glistening face glitter, or go for a mysterious look with face sequins and jewels. It's all you need to twinkle the night away!

Bring a little sparkle into your life!

City

Twinkle Tresses

Glam up your locks with some glitter hair gel! It's easy to make, looks good on any hairstyle, and washes out with shampoo, just like regular hair gel. So grab the glitter and go dazzle your friends!

You will need:
- hair gel
- small plate
- spoon
- fine glitter in different colors

1. Squeeze a big blob of hair gel onto the plate. Sprinkle about ½ teaspoon of glitter onto the gel. Mix well.

2. Smooth the gel all over your hair for lots of sparkle, or add just a little here and there for a touch of glamour.

Angel Face

Feeling a little washed-out? Don't be a shrinking violet! Give your face some instant pizzazz—and highlight your eyes, too—with this glittering face shimmer.

You will need:
- teaspoon
- petroleum jelly
- saucer or small plate
- fine glitter
- cotton swab

1. Scoop ½ teaspoon of petroleum jelly (such as Vaseline) onto a saucer. Add about ¼ teaspoon of fine glitter, then mix well with a cotton swab.

2. Using your finger, smooth a small dab of the mixture over your cheekbones and temples (but avoid getting too close to your eyes). Don't use too much though: The petroleum jelly is very greasy and you don't want the glitter to slide down your face!

Face Fancies

For extra-special sparkle, pop on a few face sequins. You can buy them from accessory and jewelry stores. They're just like normal sewing sequins, but without the holes.

You will need:
- petroleum jelly
- sequins

1. Dab a little petroleum jelly (such as Vaseline) where you want your glitz to go.

2. Press on the sequin and hold in place for a few seconds.

Hints

- For ultra staying power, dab on a spot of eyelash glue (available from most drugstores) instead of the jelly.

- For a total glitter look, start with the Angel Face (page 62), and then add a few sequins.

Mystic Sparkles

Want the look of an exotic princess? Just head to your nearest crafts store for colorful rhinestones (the kind with flat backs), then pop into the drugstore for eyelash glue. In a matter of minutes you'll be sparkling like royalty!

> **You will need:**
> - eyelash glue
> - colorful flat-backed rhinestones
> - eye makeup remover
> - cotton balls

1. Before you start, think carefully about where you want to place the stones. Be creative!

2. Dab a little bit of eyelash glue onto the back of the first stone. Lightly press it onto your skin. Repeat with as many stones as you want.

3. To take the rhinestones off, just put a little eye makeup remover on a cotton ball and rub gently over each stone.

You can follow all the advice in the world on how to look your best, but you're still going to find yourself in an emergency beauty situation every now and then.

Maybe you're going to a party and you wake up with a giant pimple. Or you're rushing to meet friends after playing basketball and there's no time to wash your hair. Perhaps your skin is shining like a pair of well-polished shoes, or you've just tried plucking your eyebrows for the first time and it looks as though you used a lawn mower.

The secret is not to panic! Just keep these emergency tips in a safe place and they will help you get through the meanest of bad beauty days.

Emergency!

Lackluster Locks

Oily, dirty hair and no time to wash it? Shake a little baby powder onto your hands and run them through your hair. Brush through until all the white disappears and you can face the world without the oil. **Try it,** this really works!

Eyebrow Catastrophe

You thought you'd try plucking your eyebrows, but the more you plucked, the more uneven they became. **STOP RIGHT THERE!**

To start with, it's best not to go attacking your brows. One or two stray hairs can go, but only pluck below the brows (never above) or they will lose their natural shape.

If you gave it a try but it went a bit wrong, just run an eyebrow pencil lightly over any bare spots to hide them. No one will know, and your brows will grow back in no time!

Hint

Try not to brush your hair too much or play with it while you're in class. This will stimulate the oil glands in your scalp (yuck!) and they'll produce more oil, making your hair even greasier.

Out-of-control Curls

If you're about to run out the door and your hair is starting to frizz, rub a drop of hand lotion between your hands and then smooth it over your hair to calm it back down.

Limp Hair

If you have fine hair that lacks body, it can be an uphill battle to keep the oomph in it. Here is a neat trick that will work for medium to long hair. Bend over and lightly spritz your upside-down hair with hair spray. When you stand up, you'll have instant body. This will also work for short hair if you want a messy, tousled look.

Hints

Here are a couple more hints for fine hair:

• Don't use too much mousse or hair spray. A little goes a long way, and too much can weigh your hair down. One little spritz of spray or a small blob of mousse is plenty.

• Once you've finished blow-drying your hair, leave it alone. Running a comb or brush through it will only weaken its shape.

Build-up Remover

Washed your hair as usual but it still looks limp and dull? It's probably because all the products you use (such as conditioner, hair spray, gel, and mousse) can build up in your hair, and shampooing doesn't always get them out. Try this quick rinse to clean your hair of all the gunk.

You will need:
- 2 cups (500 ml) warm water
- ½ cup (125 ml) fresh lemon juice
- bowl

1. Mix together the water and juice in the bowl. Lean over a sink or the tub and pour the mixture over your hair. Massage it in gently and leave it for about 15 minutes. (Have a soak in the tub while you wait.)

2. Rinse well, then admire your clean, shiny locks.

Dreaded Dandruff Herbal Rinse

Most of us have had dandruff at one time or another and it can be so embarrassing, especially if you like wearing black! Try this herbal rinse to get rid of the shoulder snow. (It might smell a bit, so avoid using this recipe just before going out.)

1. Put the ingredients in the bowl and microwave on high for 1 minute at a time until it begins to boil. Then heat on medium for 5 more minutes. If using the stove, place ingredients in the saucepan and bring to a boil over high heat. Then turn heat down and simmer (keep at a low, gentle boil) for 5 more minutes.

2. Let the mixture cool, then strain it through the sieve into the bowl.

3. Wash your hair as usual, then massage the solution into your scalp. Let it dry without rinsing.

Refresher Mist

Okay, so you've been running around all day, you get home late, and you're due to meet your friends in half an hour. You feel grubby but there's no time to shower. Try this quick body spray and soon you'll feel fresh as a daisy.

You will need:
- ½ cup (125 ml) water
- 3 drops rosewater or your favorite perfume
- spray bottle

1. Pour the water into the spray bottle. Drop in the perfume or rosewater.

2. Shake well, then spritz your face and body. Keep the spray bottle in the fridge and shake before each use.

Zits Happen

If you've found yourself with a particularly gruesome pimple, dab a little toothpaste (yes, toothpaste!) on it, which will dry it out overnight.

Cool

Make some pretty containers to keep your beauty secrets safe.

You will need something special in which to keep all the fabulous potions, perfumes, and lotions you have made. It's easy to perk up a plain bottle or add a little razzle-dazzle to an ordinary shoe box. Look to the kitchen for inspiration and collect little glass jars and bottles

Containers

with screw tops. Next, raid your closet for boxes big and small that can be used to store makeup, hairbrushes, jewelry, and accessories. Once you're stocked with containers, check out the Serious Stuff! (pages 10-11) to learn how to clean and sterilize them. Now you're ready to decorate!

Magical Makeup-Brush Holder

This cool container looks like a designer accessory, but couldn't be easier to make. With just two glasses and some tiny beads, you'll have a makeup-brush holder that looks like a million dollars.

1. Place the small container inside the larger one. Make sure there is an equal amount of space between the edges.

2. Carefully pour the colored beads into the gap left between the two glasses.

3. It's as simple as that! You're finished...unless you are the accident-prone type. Then you should go on to step 4.

4. To seal the container so the beads can't escape if you knock it over, cover the gap between the glasses with double-sided tape. Then stick some pretty ribbon over the tape.

Hint
Buy beads in slightly different colors and layer them on top of each other—for example, a layer of dark purple, followed by light purple, purply pink, and light pink.

Sparkle Jars

You'll be amazed at what a difference a little glitter can make to plain glass or plastic containers. Raid the kitchen and bathroom for screw-top jars and bottles. You won't want to keep tiny amounts of perfume in a pickle jar, so also look for travel-size plastic bottles—the kind that hold just enough shampoo for a short trip.

Clean and dry your jars thoroughly (see Serious Stuff! on pages 10-11), then get glittering! If you're short on time, you can buy glitter glue from a crafts store and just squeeze it right onto the jar or bottle. But you can be more exact with the brush and glue method given here.

You will need:

- small paintbrush
- glue or clear nail polish
- old newspaper
- jar or bottle with screw-on lid
- glitter

1. Dip the paintbrush in a little of the glue or polish, then paint a heart shape on the jar. (Don't worry if the heart shape isn't perfect!) Fill in the shape with glue or polish.

2. Before the glue or polish dries, hold the jar over some newspaper and sprinkle glitter over the heart shape.

3. Repeat with more hearts until your plain jar is a sparkly success!

Hints

- Before you start, practice different designs on paper. Stripes and dots always look great!

- If you make a mistake while painting, just wipe off the glitter quickly, before the glue dries.

- Try adding designs with glitter nail polish for a subtle, glistening effect.

Bejeweled Jars

It's easy to spruce up plain glass jars with bright, flat-backed glass beads. This simple technique works best on square jars with flat sides as the beads stick better. You can find flat-backed beads in tons of bright and beautiful colors at art and crafts stores. Even with nothing in them, these bottles are gorgeous! Place them on a sunny windowsill so the light shines through and makes the beads sparkle.

1. Place a small dab of superglue on the flat side of one of the beads, then press it onto the glass jar. Hold in place for a few seconds.

2. Stand back and decide where you want your next bead to go, then apply it in the same way. Continue until your jar is completely decorated.

Serious Stuff!

You'll need strong glue to stick the beads to the jars, so ask an adult for help. You don't want to stick yourself to the kitchen table!

Bangle Box

Cover the base and lid of a box with wrapping paper, just as if you were wrapping a present. Voilà, a gorgeous box for storing accessories or makeup!

Hint

For extra glamour, cut a length of feather trim long enough to fit around the top of the box. Attach with double-sided tape.

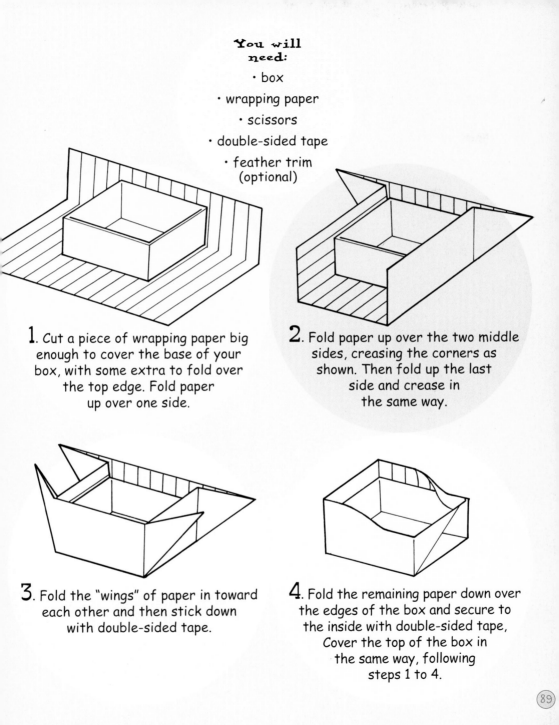

- box
- wrapping paper
- scissors
- double-sided tape
- feather trim
(optional)

1. Cut a piece of wrapping paper big enough to cover the base of your box, with some extra to fold over the top edge. Fold paper up over one side.

2. Fold paper up over the two middle sides, creasing the corners as shown. Then fold up the last side and crease in the same way.

3. Fold the "wings" of paper in toward each other and then stick down with double-sided tape.

4. Fold the remaining paper down over the edges of the box and secure to the inside with double-sided tape, Cover the top of the box in the same way, following steps 1 to 4.

Love and Kisses

Cut out lots of different-sized heart shapes from two colors of paper, then glue them onto a box, overlapping the hearts until you can't see any of the box underneath.

Another idea is to cut out photos of your favorite celebs from magazines and stick these on instead. As well as being a cool container for jewelry or hair clips, this makes a great gift box!

You will need:

- box with lid
- Colored paper or pages from an old issue of your favorite magazine
- pen or pencil
- scissors
- glue
- pom-pom (optional)

1. Draw heart-shape patterns in two or three different sizes. Cut them out.

2. Use the patterns to trace as many hearts as you think you will need to cover your box, then cut them all out.

3. Glue the hearts onto your box, overlapping each shape until the box is entirely covered. If you like, glue a pom-pom onto the top for a finishing touch.

Hints

- Cut out pictures of your favorite celebs and cover a box with them.

- For mother's day or your mom's birthday, find pictures of her favorite flowers and use them to cover a beautiful gift box for her.

Box of Trix

Turn an old box into a thing of beauty that will brighten up your bedroom and keep your makeup in apple-pie order. It's easy to do—all you need are some strips of colored ribbon and tissue paper. So unleash your creative side and get wrapping!

1. Cover the base and the lid of your gift box with your chosen paper (see how in Bangle Box, page 89).

2. Cut lengths of colored ribbon, each long enough to cover the top and sides of the lid, plus some extra to tuck inside. Cut enough lengths to cover the lid.

3. Turn the lid over. Take your first ribbon length and, using double-sided tape, stick one end of it to the inside of the lid at one corner. Pass the ribbon over the top of the lid and attach the other end to the inside of the opposite corner.

4. Repeat step 3 with different colors of ribbon until you have covered the box lid.

5. Cut a length of ribbon to fit around the base of the box. Wrap it around the sides and secure it at the front with double-sided tape.

6. Tie a bow from leftover ribbon, then use it to cover the tape from step 5, securing it with double-sided tape.

Hot Tip

Before you start, cut the ribbon lengths and lay them across the lid to plan where you're going to stick them. If you have space left over (but not enough room for another ribbon), leave an equal gap at each edge.

Stick-on Style

For a quick and easy project, buy a strip of sparkly stickers and use them to cover a small box. If you don't have that many stickers, cover the box in plain-colored paper (see Bangle Box, page 89), then add a few shiny stickers on the top to brighten it up.

Funky Junk

Instead of tossing old magazines, flip through them and cut out pics of cute boys, cartoons, or anything else you like. Then use your scraps to cover an old drinking glass or jar. You'll end up with a cool comb and brush holder, pencil holder, makeup-brush holder—in fact, an anything-tall-and-thin holder!

You will need:
- clean drinking glass or jar
- pictures from magazines
- scissors
- glue
- small paintbrush

1. Make sure the glass or jar is clean and dry. Use the paintbrush to cover the back of one of your scraps with glue, then stick it onto the glass.

2. Keep pasting and sticking pictures on, overlapping them as you go, until the whole glass is covered. When you come to the top and base of the glass, just fold over the picture onto the bottom or inside the top for a great finish.

Index of Recipes and Ingredients